NATIONAL GEOGRAPHIC

Ladders

ONWARD!

Bottom of the World

by Michael Bilski

Imagine a place that gets less than an inch of **precipitation** a year. That's hardly any drizzle, rain, snow, or sleet. There are icy mountains over three miles high. The average **temperature** during the coldest month is between –40°F and –94°F (–40°C and –70°C). Now that is cold! What and where is this place? It is the **continent** of Antarctica. It's the land of the **South Pole.** This is the frozen desert at the bottom of the world.

Haiku 1

Bottom of the world

Continent like no other

Stark Antarctica!

Haiku 2

World's coldest desert

Freezing in the ice and wind

Is it ever warm?

Haiku 3

Lure to explorers

Brave men who would not give up

Onward to the Pole!

Check In How would you describe Antarctica?

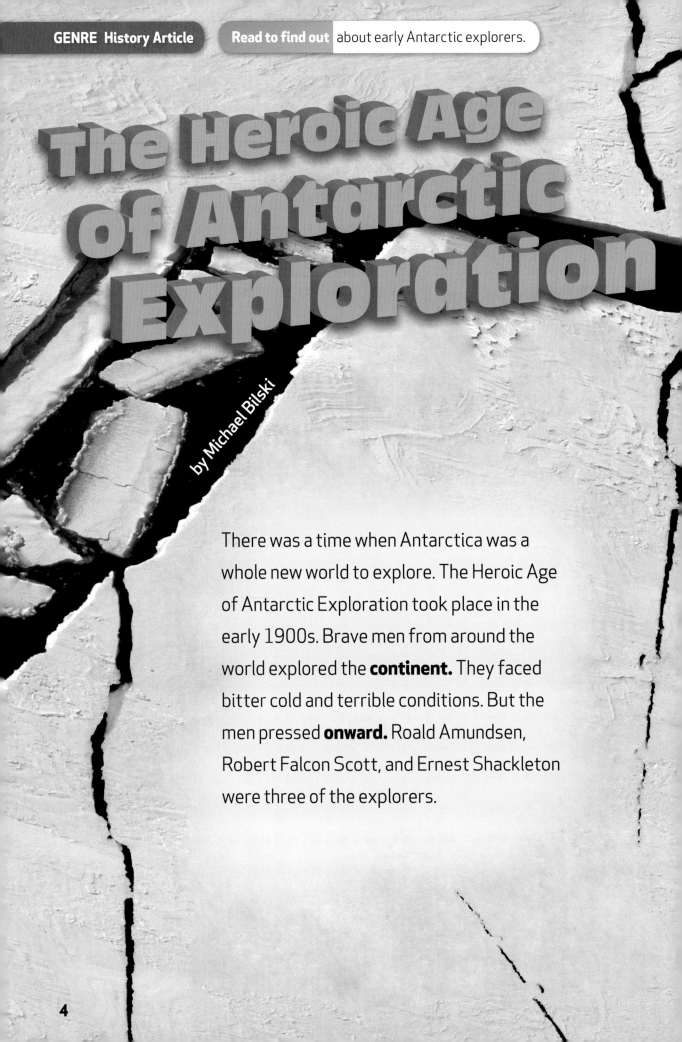

The Heroic Age of Antarctic Exploration

by Michael Bilski

There was a time when Antarctica was a whole new world to explore. The Heroic Age of Antarctic Exploration took place in the early 1900s. Brave men from around the world explored the **continent.** They faced bitter cold and terrible conditions. But the men pressed **onward.** Roald Amundsen, Robert Falcon Scott, and Ernest Shackleton were three of the explorers.

Antarctic Explorers

Erich von Drygalski

German South Polar
Expedition, 1901–1903

Roald Amundsen

Norwegian Antarctic
Expedition, 1910–1912

*First to reach South Pole
(December 14, 1911)*

Adriene de Gerlache

Belgian Antarctic
Expedition, 1897–1899

William Speirs Bruce

Scottish National
Antarctic Expedition,
1902–1904

Ernest Shackleton

British Antarctic
Expedition, 1907–1909

Imperial Trans-Antarctic
Expedition, 1914–1917

Shackleton-Rowett
Expedition, 1921–1922

**Carsten
Borchgrevink**

British Antarctic
Expedition, 1898–1900

Jean-Baptiste Charcot

French Antarctic
Expedition, 1903–1905
and 1908–1910

Nobu Shirase

Japanese Antarctic
Expedition, 1910–1912

**Nils Otto
Nordenskjold**

Swedish South Polar
Expedition, 1901–1903

Robert Falcon Scott

British National Antarctic
Expedition, 1901–1904

British Antarctic
Expedition, 1910–1913

*Reached South Pole
(January 17, 1912)*

Douglas Mawson

Australasian Antarctic
Expedition, 1911–1914

Roald Amundsen

Roald Amundsen was born in Norway in 1872. He explored the Arctic. There, Amundsen learned how the Inuit survived. He wore reindeer clothing and learned about using sled dogs. Amundsen wanted to be the first to reach the **North Pole.** But other explorers reached the North Pole first. So Amundsen decided that he would be the first to reach the **South Pole.** He knew that Robert Scott had the same goal. The race was on!

Robert Falcon Scott

Robert Falcon Scott was born in England in 1868. He had a career in the navy. Scott's first **expedition** to Antarctica took place from 1901 to 1904. Scott and his team came within 400 miles of the South Pole. Scott was determined to lead the first expedition to reach the South Pole. He went back to Antarctica in 1911. Scott knew that Amundsen had the same goal, but Scott would not give up.

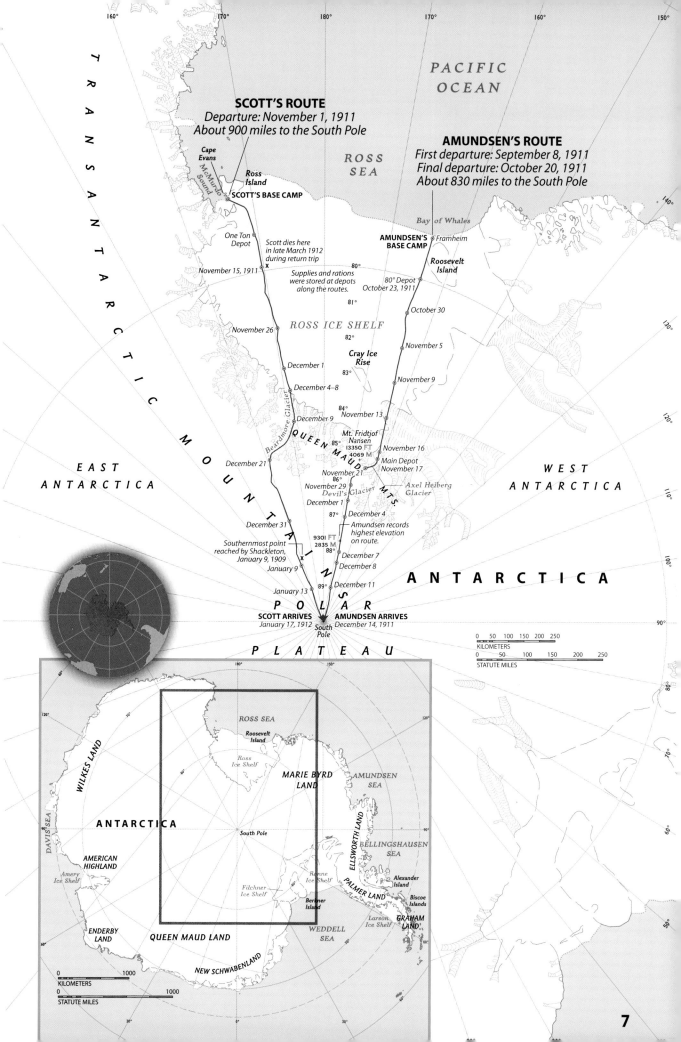

PACIFIC
OCEAN

SCOTT'S ROUTE
*Departure: November 1, 1911
About 900 miles to the South Pole*

ROSS
SEA

AMUNDSEN'S ROUTE
*First departure: September 8, 1911
Final departure: October 20, 1911
About 830 miles to the South Pole*

Cape
Evans
*Ross
Island*
SCOTT'S BASE CAMP

Bay of Whales

*One Ton
Depot*

*Scott dies here
in late March 1912
during return trip*
x

AMUNDSEN'S
BASE CAMP
Framheim

November 15, 1911

80°

*Supplies and rations
were stored at depots
along the routes.*

*Roosevelt
Island*

*80° Depot
October 23, 1911*

81°

October 30

November 26

ROSS ICE SHELF

82°

November 5

*Cray Ice
Rise*

December 1

83°

November 9

December 4–8

84°

November 13

December 9

*Mt. Fridtjof
Nansen*
13350 FT
4069 M
+

EAST
ANTARCTICA

85°

November 16

WEST
ANTARCTICA

December 21

*Main Depot
November 17*

86°

November 21

November 29

Devil's Glacier

*Axel Heiberg
Glacier*

December 1

87°

December 4

December 31

*Amundsen records
highest elevation
on route.*

9301 FT
2835 M
88°

*Southernmost point
reached by Shackleton,
January 9, 1909*
x

December 7

January 9

December 8

POLAR

89°

December 11

ANTARCTICA

January 13

SCOTT ARRIVES
January 17, 1912

South
Pole

AMUNDSEN ARRIVES
December 14, 1911

PLATEAU

0 50 100 150 200 250
KILOMETERS
0   50   100   150   200   250
STATUTE MILES

ANTARCTICA

ROSS SEA

Roosevelt
Island

Ross
Ice Shelf

WILKES
LAND

MARIE BYRD
LAND

AMUNDSEN
SEA

ANTARCTICA

ELLSWORTH LAND

BELLINGSHAUSEN
SEA

DAVIS
SEA

South Pole

AMERICAN
HIGHLAND

Amery
Ice Shelf

Ronne
Ice Shelf

Alexander
Island

PALMER LAND

Biscoe
Islands

ENDERBY
LAND

Filchner
Ice Shelf

Berkner
Island

WEDDELL
SEA

Larson
Ice Shelf

GRAHAM
LAND

QUEEN MAUD LAND

NEW SCHWABENLAND

0   1000
KILOMETERS
0   1000
STATUTE MILES

7

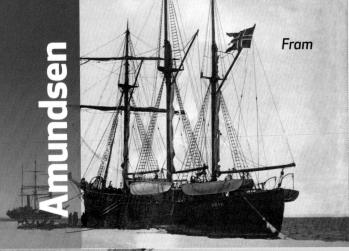

Fram

Amundsen

The Pole Is the Goal

Amundsen and Scott shared a goal. Each wanted to be the first explorer to reach the South Pole. Who would win the race?

On January 3, 1911, Scott and his **crew** arrived in Antarctica on their ship, *Terra Nova*. They lost some cargo during a storm at sea, but Scott's team still arrived with many dogs, ponies, and gasoline-powered sleds. Scott and his men set up **depots** to store food and supplies along the way to the South Pole. But one of the sleds broke down, and the ponies struggled in the bitter cold. The team could not set up their main depot as far south as they had hoped.

Terra Nova

Scott

Sled at a supply depot

On January 14, 1911, Amundsen and his crew arrived in Antarctica on their ship, *Fram*. They set up camp on the Ross Ice Shelf. They spent nine months getting ready for their trip to the South Pole.

Amundsen was prepared. He remembered what he had learned from the Inuit. He brought almost 100 sled dogs to Antarctica. He brought supplies, food, and fresh water, too. Amundsen and his crew set up depots with food along the way to the Pole. The men practiced and prepared as they waited for the warmer spring weather. They trained the dogs. They practiced skiing. The men used the trained dogs and sleds to get their depots closer to the Pole than Scott could. Amundsen made sure his men and dogs were well-fed and well-rested for the trip ahead.

Dog team

Testing the sea's depth
with a hammer

Amundsen's team
at the South Pole

Victory and Defeat

Amundsen left for the South Pole on October 20, 1911.
His crew included a champion skier and two expert dog
drivers. They took four sleds and more than 50 dogs. The
food depots did the trick. The men skied and the dogs pulled
the sleds. They climbed mountains and battled blizzards.
But the men and dogs pressed onward. Finally, on December
14, 1911, they reached the Pole! There was no sign of Scott.
The race was won. Amundsen and his men celebrated. They
planted a flag and set up a tent. Amundsen left a note for
Scott inside the tent.

Scott and his crew left base camp on November 1, 1911.
They took 10 ponies, sleds, and more than 20 dogs. The
gasoline-powered sleds failed and the ponies struggled. The
team faced bitter cold, ice, and snow. A blizzard stopped
them for four days.

Both explorers chose their teams and equipment differently.

AMUNDSEN'S TEAM   ■ Survived trip   □ Did not survive

SCOTT'S TEAM

As planned, these men turned back
before reaching the South Pole.

The total number of sleds is uncertain. Two
were brought back by returning men.

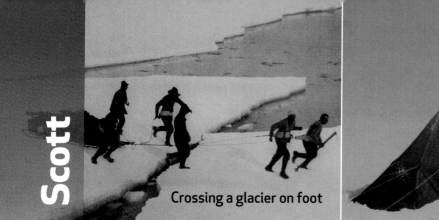
Scott

Crossing a glacier on foot

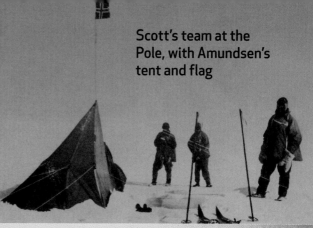
Scott's team at the Pole, with Amundsen's tent and flag

Scott's team had to march on foot toward the South Pole. They were not good skiers, and they had to pull their own sleds. Scott sent the dogs and most of the men back to camp. He decided to take four men the rest of the way. On January 16, 1912, they saw Amundsen's tent and flag in the distance. They knew they had lost the race. They reached the South Pole the next day. In the tent, they found Amundsen's note and some much-needed supplies.

Amundsen and his team had made it back safely. Scott's team was not as lucky. They were starving, ill, and tired. The remaining men were trapped by a blizzard. They were just 11 miles from their largest depot. They never made it there. Scott's diary entry finished the sad story.

"We shall stick it out to the end, but we are getting weaker, of course, and the end cannot be far. It seems a pity, but I do not think I can write more."

All surviving dogs were brought back by returning team members.

Shackleton's Endurance

Sled dogs watch *Endurance* sink.

Ernest Henry Shackleton

Ernest Henry Shackleton was born in 1874 in Ireland. He was a member of Scott's crew during Scott's first trip to the South Pole in 1901. Shackleton led his own expedition in 1908. He set a record by getting closer to the South Pole than anyone had before that time.

Amundsen won the race to the South Pole. So Shackleton decided to try something new. He would cross Antarctica on foot. His expedition would start at the Weddell Sea

This map traces their route.

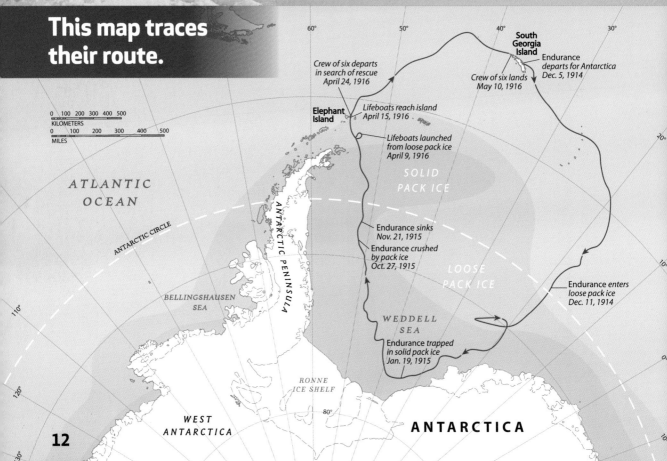

and cross a part of Antarctica that had never been explored. Then he would head to the Pole and to the Ross Sea.

Shackleton and his men spotted Antarctica from their ship, *Endurance*. But before they got there, *Endurance* became trapped in a drifting pack ice. It was a fatal blow to the expedition. The ship was trapped for ten long months. Meanwhile Shackleton and his men used *Endurance* to store their supplies. But the ice was slowly crushing the doomed ship. Supplies and lifeboats had to be removed. On November 21, 1915, *Endurance* was crushed and later sank.

Shackleton and his crew drifted on the pack ice for another five months. They endured bitter cold. They survived partly on whale and seal meat. Shackleton's men were finally able to escape the ice in their lifeboats. They got safely to Elephant Island.

Shackleton and his men were trapped on the ice. They didn't set foot on land for more than a year.

Shackleton decided the only hope for rescue was to sail one of the lifeboats to the nearest inhabited island. It was a dangerous mission. With a crew of five men, Shackleton sailed 800 miles to South Georgia Island. They found a ship that could bring them back to rescue the rest of the crew. After several tries, every member of Shackleton's expedition was rescued on August 30, 1916. The men had been away from home for more than two years. The expedition was a failure, but the story of *Endurance* had a heroic end. Shackleton and his fellow explorers had endured.

In 1921 Shackleton reunited with some members of the *Endurance* crew. The plan was to sail a new ship, *Quest*, around Antarctica. Shackleton had a heart attack while on board *Quest*. He was buried on South Georgia Island.

Shackleton's crew on board *Quest*

End of the Heroic Age

This heroic age ended with Shackleton's death. The final continent had been explored. Both Amundsen and Scott had reached the South Pole. Exploration of a different kind continues to this day. Scientists from all over the world have set up research stations to study this frozen land.

Endurance

Check In   What did Scott, Amundsen, and Shackleton have in common? How were they different?

Andrew
Evans

Meet Andrew Evans, National Geographic's "Digital Nomad." A nomad is a traveler. Andrew is a digital nomad. He uses technology to communicate about his travels.

Andrew was like the explorers of the Heroic Age of Antarctic Exploration. He wanted to explore **Antarctica**. But instead of sailing there, he traveled most of the way by bus. People followed Andrew's journey on his **blog**. He posted news for them every day.

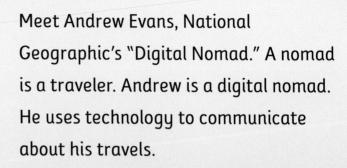

Andrew's Antarctic Adventure

by Michael Bilski

Tools

In the first decades of the 20th century, the explorers Amundsen, Scott, and Shackleton used navigation instruments. A compass and a sextant helped them find their way toward the **South Pole**. They recorded their journeys using large box cameras.

Andrew and other explorers today have tools that use GPS, or "Global Positioning System." GPS receivers, digital cameras, and the Internet help explorers find their way and keep a record of their journey. Andrew travels light, but he always takes small cameras with him, including a waterproof one.

Present	Past
 Cell-phone compass	 Compass
 GPS receiver	 Sextant
 Waterproof camera	 Box camera

Heading South

Andrew got on the bus on January 1, 2010. He left from the National Geographic offices in Washington, DC. Before beginning his journey, Andrew had asked blog readers to help him pick songs. The songs helped pass the time on the long bus ride.

ATLANTIC OCEAN

The first place Andrew visited in South America was Cartagena, Colombia. Cartagena has narrow, cobbled streets and old Spanish buildings. Every house, door, and shutter is a different color.

VENEZUELA

COLOMBIA

ECUADOR

PERU

BRAZIL

UNITED STATES

MEXICO

BELIZE

GUATEMALA **HONDURAS**

EL SALVADOR **NICARAGUA**

COSTA RICA **PANAMA**

In Costa Rica, Andrew saw mountain streams, macaws, toucans, and crocodiles from his bus window.

Andrew had hoped to see sunny beaches along the Mexican coastline. But rain made the beaches gray and colorless. Andrew did see white egrets and purple-black grackles.

The road in and out of La Paz, Bolivia, was over 13,500 feet in elevation. That's more than two miles high! Andrew saw the Uyuni salt flats in Southern Bolivia. They make up the world's largest salt desert.

URUGUAY

PARAG

BOLIVIA

ARGENTINA

CHILE

PACIFIC OCEAN

Andrew crossed the **Equator** in Ecuador. He walked along the line between North and South. He had one foot in each hemisphere.

Andrew crossed the border from Ecuador to Peru and the land changed from a tropical jungle to a desert. Here the Sechura Desert meets the Pacific Ocean to the west. It meets the Andes Mountains to the east.

The final bus ride went through Argentina. Andrew traveled more than 3100 miles. He passed through Cordoba, then **onward** to Ushuaia in Tierra del Fuego. The Strait of Magellan was rough. That made the short ferry ride scary.

Antarctica at Last

No more buses! Andrew boarded the *MV National Geographic Explorer* to sail to Antarctica. A highlight was seeing a pod of fin whales in front of the ship. Andrew saw his first iceberg, too.

ATLANTIC OCEAN

ARGENTINA

CHILE

ANTARCTICA

Andrew set foot on Antarctica. Its natural beauty touched him. He felt happy that he could leave his boot prints on the soil of the seventh **continent**.

Andrew visited Deception Island. It's a volcanic crown hollowed out from the inside. The whole island is the mouth of a volcano. On the beach, Andrew went for a swim. Since the water was 36°F (2°C), he didn't stay in long.

On South Georgia Island, Andrew took this picture of a very rare all-black penguin. Its coloring is called melanism. Melanism happens when the body has extra melanin. This makes skin, fur, or feathers dark.

The rules for visitors to Antarctica say that you cannot touch any wildlife. You must stay 15 feet away from the animals at all times. But at the Gentoo penguin colony, a baby penguin jumped into Andrew's lap. Then another one came. It was all he could do to obey the rules and not cuddle the penguins.

PACIFIC OCEAN

Andrew traveled through 14 countries. He covered 10,000 miles in 10 weeks! His trip began on a bus in Washington, DC. It ended on the continent of Antarctica.

Like the explorers of the Heroic Age of Antarctic Exploration, Andrew set his sights on a destination. He dealt with bumps along the way, but he pressed onward. It's what explorers do.

Check In What did you find most interesting about Andrew's trip?

1. What do you think connects the three pieces that you read in this book? What makes you think that?

2. Compare and contrast the reasons why Amundsen, Scott, Shackleton, and Evans went to Antarctica. How were their reasons alike and different?

3. Andrew Evans uses modern tools, such as a GPS device and a cell phone. How might modern tools have changed the other explorers' expeditions?

4. Choose a haiku. Then find a passage or a photo in another piece that explains or shows what the haiku is describing. Tell how they are connected.

5. What questions do you still wonder about Antarctica or its explorers?